Additional praise for *Abscission*:

Kathy Alma Peterson's beautiful elegiac book, *Abscission*, explores what it means to be human, to suffer the loss of a partner, and to attempt to come to terms with mortality or as the title suggests, that final detachment. Peterson is both a poet and a painter and she employs rich imagery throughout. For example, how remarkable to write " The afterlife, formless and colorless, / approximates a charcoal drawing of a decimated forest." In the poem "Ventriloquist," Peterson lays bare a heart "encouraging the irises / to breathe into another day," as if to ward off grief, even temporarily. But this is also a voice unflinching in its struggle to reconcile personal sorrow " I see his face, no longer aging like my own," against the vastness of the greater journey " think of the living / as limited to bargains of / continuance, an afterlife wherein / something is made of them, a place better than a planet / which forces them to leave it." Peterson's voice rises out of quiet musings and acute observation, as in her opening poem "Night Sky," which concludes in painterly fashion " Thoughts are fireflies and reality is the night sky," and in her last and title poem "Abscission," in which the speaker states "As a leaf myself I sometimes wish / to be glued to the mother-branch / knowing I will detach, float, and glow." These astonishing poems read like finely cut jewels, spare, concise, and achingly mined.
 —Babo Kamel

K. Alma Peterson transforms *Abscission*, a botanical term meaning the normal separation of flowers and fruit, into the fraught arena of a beloved's death. Abounding with an admirable wildness, the poems in this collection show how far one must bend in the midst of a paralyzing grief: "touch a stone, then / his skin, then a curtain / of solitude. . ." The atonality of grief governs with an "atmospheric sorrow [which] leaves/the ocean colorless," and even the afterlife "approximates a charcoal drawing of a decimated forest." In poems that juxtapose the range of human activity—from jackpots in a casino stirring the blood ("Casino With Open Access to the Natural World") to a reality in which there's "nothing like/face time with a seagull," Peterson charts the business of living in the mist of catastrophic loss. What's at stake in these poems is nothing less than the entire range of being: "from a single seed / begins a tree's full life / crown shaped like clouds / paraphrasing sky"
 —John Minczeski

Abscission

poems by

K. Alma Peterson

Finishing Line Press
Georgetown, Kentucky

Abscission

Copyright © 2026 by K. Alma Peterson
ISBN 979-8-89990-373-1 First Edition
All rights reserved under International and Pan-American Copyright Conventions. No part of this book may be reproduced in any manner whatsoever without written permission from the publisher, except in the case of brief quotations embodied in critical articles and reviews.

ACKNOWLEDGMENTS

A sincere thank you, and acknowledgment to the journals who have shown the following poems:
Raven Review, April 2024, "Meeting."
EcoTheo, Spring 2024, "Detachment."
Delmarva Review, March 2023, Volume 16, "The Whereabouts of One Who Ceases to Be."
Delmarva Review, March 2023, Volume 16, "Kite."
Delmarva Review, March 2023, Volume 16, "Cadence."
EcoTheo, Spring 2024, "Abscission."
The Cafe Review, Spring 2025, "Night Sky"
Midway Journal, Volume 19 - Issue 1, "[   ]"

Publisher: Leah Huete de Maines
Editor: Christen Kincaid
Cover Art: Kathy (K. Alma) Peterson
Author Photo: Kathy (K. Alma) Peterson
Cover Design: Elizabeth Maines McCleavy

Order online: www.finishinglinepress.com
also available on amazon.com

Author inquiries and mail orders:
Finishing Line Press
PO Box 1626
Georgetown, Kentucky 40324
USA

Contents

Night Sky 1
Meeting 2
Detachment 3
Live Oak 4
On Melancholia 5
Verses from the Earth 6
Ventriloquist 7
Often Through Solitude 8
Casino With Open Access to the Natural World 9
The Whereabouts of One Who Ceases to Be 10
Kite 11
Grief 12
Adjournment 13
Accountability 14
Cadence 15
"Enough Light?" 16
Derivations of Dusk 17
Steady State 18
At Sunset 19
Caesura 20
We're Over Here 21
[   ] 22
Abscission 23

*"...So it is better to speak
remembering
we were never meant to survive."*

—Audre Lorde from "A Litany for Survival"

Night Sky

Waiting for dark to simplify my view

I stand and study wild quinine in the meadow
its bright white flowers bear upon resilience.

Bluestem grasses sweep and swerve between

bursts of lupine cropping up like decades-old
conversations, images of what we wore, where

we drove, when I knew you were my ground.

It all takes place on this heath of consciousness:
swales where details flatten like blown grasses,

where petals plucked declare the place and time

where loss provoked was loss sustained,
memory mistaken for something hard-and-fast.

Thoughts are fireflies and reality is the night sky.

Meeting

Her house was full of the dead
and nowhere were the quick
so quick to tell me their sweat
was from the exertion it took
to stay alive. She'd been dead
a month, and earlier, onshore,
I ran (I cannot run) along the long
prelude to sensation: cool water
on my doubts. These were
my loved ones, simultaneously
alive and dead, touching my skin,
explaining why many layers were needed.
Some bodies resisted long and hard
more than one of themselves, never mind
the house full of snakes shedding
memories of other rivers,

Detachment

I'm falling out of love with the ocean, there
to swallow me in one swell of its incessant rhythm.

When I dissolve to one energetic drop, the sea
will claim me, in accordance with metaphysical law,

water to water, a layer of dust my remnant on the landscape.

My idea of beauty has begun to shift to vultures
in dead trees, abandoned buildings, stones worn down

by aforementioned ocean. The afterlife, formless and colorless,
approximates a charcoal drawing of a decimated forest,

outer space enlarged, with figments of imagined waves.

Live Oak

born to a branch
a leaf in slowest motion
twirls and uncurls from
a reluctant bud

attached to a trunk
a branch for a lifetime
scrapes a near window
when winds write

like investigative roots
a trunk until its demise
by destruction or disease
weaves through the air

from a tiny seedling
roots extend and expand
as deep into the ground
as topography allows

from a single seed
begins a tree's full life
crown shaped like clouds
paraphrasing sky

On Melancholia

-1-

a stream deep for its width   the haunt
of an idler alone on its bank

grasses matted   by animals resting
drinking their fill   scared off by the form

and vibe of a woman   her aura
a fringe snarled and knotted

reeking of sorrows

-2-

fraught with her wrong   response to
devotion   preserving what little

might matter to memory

rain relieves   her obligation to feign
joy as if it can be

she watches the heron   wading
alone on the shoreline   envies its slow

up and away

Verses From the Earth

…/ we are trending in the limelight to tweet the color green

…/ in the moat of loneliness swim rescue teams of manatees
…/ maintenance of the drawbridge falls to extroverts with red paint

…/ left to our own devotions we beseech the beech invoke the oak
…/ we delve and dive for words to inspire better Earthkeeping

…/ we manifest our genes the way the lake reflects the trees
…/ lest we portray the sky dark we clean our cloudy brushes

…/ what we fear losing hurries to make its disappearance

…/ of great amusement to the trees we claim to put down roots
…/ our totem tree holds the heron that will carry us away

…/ in the time remaining collect your toys and tools to trade
…/ to the memory of your work may the bees thrive & buzz

Ventriloquist

Doing its best
to revive the cut flowers
in the blue vase
in the other room
the heart throws its pulse
into the quiet night air
encouraging the irises
to breathe into another
day before they're soggy
to the point of dropping
to the floor their last
whisper attaching to
the ear a distant echo
of color and sound
brought in from the out
of doors to endure
for the remainder
of their lush life-form
contained in water
listening to the heart-voice.

Often Through Solitude

She remembers her heartlessness
cringes at her disregard, well aware,
were it possible to turn back time,
she would repeat herself, the self
whose shadow was absolved for
its wrongdoing. The shadow, episodic
in its discontent, high and shifting
shape in an effort to escape itself—

Years fall like night; the shadow's reach
retreats. Like noon sun, remorse burns
a steady imprint of the damage done:
revisions can't be written but the story's
true side brings to light the liminal ground—
less harsh reflection of what's been.

Casino With Open Access to the Natural World

The river and the forest
are surroundings.

The grip of chance and commerce
never loosens.

The casino never closes.
Neither does the ocean, marsh or meadow.

Sunsets don't take tokens.
Jackpots stir the blood but there's nothing like

face time with a seagull.
A poker face won't coax the otter

onto a riverbank. In the forest
there is no such thing as money growing.

Moss covers all coinage.
You won't see any birds in the casino.

How do clouds keep winning
so much rain?

The Whereabouts of One Who Ceases to Be

He took a drive in his preferred conveyance,
absorbing the small pleasures in his surroundings.
He arrived at a location in the minds of those
who will think of him, remember there was music playing, or

silence if a breezy early evening was its own song.
In his year in the passing lane, he taught the wind
to wear his words like a fleece vest on chilly mornings.
Then he closed the window to hear himself think

something other than entrapment in a body of no use
to the space it occupied—his captor in matters
of remaining time. What he thought he could have done
there was no possibility he could have done.

I see his face, no longer aging like my own.
I hear his words; a stir of air, my recognition.

Kite

His profile in the palm trees, the clouds,
from memory: suggestions of the husband
I observed browsing catalogs, soldering pieces
of stained glass into a whole. In the clear space
of windows, I see his face, filigreed lines, broken
form pleading for my company

as health took its leave of him. All I could see
was his shadow, humorless, ill at ease, an outline
of the man who stood my ground for me,
watching me investigate the eight directions
of the wind, resisting settlement. I kept
my distance and my place at the same time,
imagining a quiet landing for the kite, and him,
and me. Our fears splintered the updrafts.

Grief

The sagging shoulders of his coat
suit her failure to absolve herself—
mistaken proportions,
compulsions turned to crimes.

She befriends a long storm
cornering her house, a tidal wave
of self-blame battering the door
held open by her shadow.

She belongs to the dust
collecting and recollecting
where he sat, what he dreamt
driving into the future,
his arm around her regrets.

Adjournment

At the trailhead we paused,
knowing what was blazed
went on interminably
with choices in the arrows.

There is a room in back
of every dream, a place of rest
as if an opening in the brain
were a bridge to morning.

We rearrange the room, couch
suggestions of lucid feng shui
the way we finish each other's
color schemes, fill in memories.

Little do the memories know, skewed
as they are by contingent recollections.
Was it five days or five years
since you joined the imaginary?

Accountability

A rivulet, then
a river, then a blistered
sea: waters changing
at imposed depth and pace.

A whine, then a keen,
then sirens of emergency:
piercing sounds signal
distress, ebb of life.

I touch a stone, then
his skin, then a curtain
of solitude. All sensation
withdraws from my hands.

The silence of indifference,
then a blue that doesn't lighten.
An atmospheric sorrow leaves
the ocean colorless.

Cadence

Befriended wren, you sit
on my shoulder, and every day
I am reminded of how weightless
my life is, how little Death
will gain when it takes me
to the top of your coniferous tree,
releases me to winter clouds.

Now, guardian bird, you reside
within my rib cage, uncertain
when you might burst free—
your wingbeats with a power
equal to Death's—to tear yourself out
of the bars that are my view, my
awareness, of the final rhyme, my terror.

"Enough light?"

Every day the sunset
asks its vibrant question;
every day I answer
that I crave the darkness
hiding me from flippant
palm trees, ospreys shrieking
their rendition
of remembered glee.

I am living the late question now,
treading closing arguments
like a log-roller, every happen-step
shows one side of itself
pitching the body into chaos.

Derivations of Dusk

Gentle somewhere, find me. Come from nowhere.

At the pass, headed off. Day, already part gloaming.

Tarp of dusk billows. Bloom loose, flowering fish.

Hearten whilst we swim. Hearten me from nowhere.

Blood-headed, off we swam. Pass book overhead.

Gentle sky, flowing fish. Flower of sky.

Steady State

Leaving
the world nightly
opening the hinged gate
to a revolving hologram—
events

dislodge.
I'm at the wheel
asleep when the steering
column detaches from its dash-
board bolt.

The wheel
and I advance
at migrating bird-speed.
In transit the whirring of time
recedes.

We pass
ourselves written
on a melting glacier
in the process of erasure
gleaming.

At Sunset

Pressed down
by a wall of darkening blue
the roseate clouds seem lost in remembrance

not mourning what's elapsed, but dead certain
worlds were overlooked, a trove of skills
and secrets youth had promised

failed to take shape
before now, not pausing to be fully felt
or, in slow motion, arriving moments later

than wisdom stood in need of. Or, for that matter,
love, of the startled and grateful kind,
willing to trade

illusion for contentment,
ownership for safekeeping, all the while
a field of rose-pink clouds occupies the riven sky.

Caesura

Airwaves made visible on the water's surface;
small uncertainties nodding in my mind:

this is the distant future into which
I forwarded the unexplored questions:

trinkets in a velvet pouch, stones into the lake
after an argument, to be settled only in the depths

and over time. Where was I in our hesitance
to test the waters, and where were you, measuring

how far to the lake's opposite shore: could we
add cloud-speeds, divide by our devotion

to a stationary boat? Unconscious drives
push in all directions; we fail to admit

what we sense and can't name, the way we know
rate and time but cannot bear the distance.

We're Over Here

—think of the dead
as devoid of recollection, taken
to a dream state in a microcosm
of the cosmos, viewing their
abandoned body without a hint
of recognition or confusion,
absorbing a world where sleep
is a function of constant darkness.

—think of the living
as limited to bargains of
continuance, an afterlife wherein
something is made of them,
a place better than a planet
which forces them to leave it.

—think of dreaming
as a medium through which
wavelengths pass crest to crest
moving energy until the living
sever ties with Earth, adjoin
the next frequency of sound.

—think of traveling within
a space where motion is illusory,
where objects interact but never touch,
and body is a synonym for intangible.

[   ]

As a ghost, I explore concrete—cities mostly
where I blend with smoke, and smoke cigarettes
(nothing to lose; I am ephemeral).

Selfies only other ghosts can see—I take them
of myself with marble statues, terrazzo floors,
porcelain vases. I envy the edges of things:
corners of buildings, facial features, drops of rain.

Every chance I get, I step in a mud puddle, hoping
I will acquire some identifying feature, become
more than a spiral of wind, an ominous feeling.

My thoughts are the most solid thing about me.
I can pass them on to crowds, and no one knows
where they came from.

As a ghost, I remember my past lives, with no
means of explaining. I am Imagination, that's
as close as I get to having a name. If I envelop you
as I sometimes do in dreams, don't be afraid.
If you have an extra scarf or sweater, leave it
on the sidewalk. The halls of Memory are chilly.

When you're a ghost, you'll understand:
we represent the veil, the other side, the afterlife.

As a ghost, I miss my body. I miss my teeth,
my fingers holding a fork. I would give up
my eternity for one hour of being seen; to be
more than the chill on someone's skin.

Abscission

As a leaf myself I sometimes wish
to be glued to the mother-branch
knowing I will detach, float, and glow
briefly on the dark sidewalk,
relinquish my individuality
to the treesome Unconscious
reflecting the sky back to October.

K. Alma Peterson is a poet and painter. She resides in Florida and spends summers in her native Minnesota. Both her poetry and her painting explore abstraction and metaphorical representations of what is seen and experienced. She is a graduate of the Warren Wilson MFA Program for Writers. Her poems have appeared widely in online and print journals. Blaze Vox Books published two collections of her poetry: *Was There No Interlude When Light Sprawled the Fen* (2010) and *The Last Place I Lived* (2015).

www.ingramcontent.com/pod-product-compliance
Lightning Source LLC
Chambersburg PA
CBHW080226170426
43192CB00015B/2770